THIS IS ME!

VERSES FROM THE UK

Edited By Daisy Job

First published in Great Britain in 2022 by:

YoungWriters® Est. 1991

Young Writers
Remus House
Coltsfoot Drive
Peterborough
PE2 9BF
Telephone: 01733 890066
Website: www.youngwriters.co.uk

Book Design by Ashley Janson

Softback ISBN 978-1-80015-838-2

Printed and bound in the UK by BookPrintingUK
Website: www.bookprintinguk.com
YB0498C

FOREWORD

For Young Writers' latest competition This Is Me, we asked primary school pupils to look inside themselves, to think about what makes them unique, and then write a poem about it! They rose to the challenge magnificently and the result is this fantastic collection of poems in a variety of poetic styles.

Here at Young Writers our aim is to encourage creativity in children and to inspire a love of the written word, so it's great to get such an amazing response, with some absolutely fantastic poems. It's important for children to focus on and celebrate themselves and this competition allowed them to write freely and honestly, celebrating what makes them great, expressing their hopes and fears, or simply writing about their favourite things. This Is Me gave them the power of words. The result is a collection of inspirational and moving poems that also showcase their creativity and writing ability.

I'd like to congratulate all the young poets in this anthology, I hope this inspires them to continue with their creative writing.

CONTENTS

Didcot Primary Academy, Didcot

Edderton Primary School, Tain

Evendons Primary School, Wokingham

THE POEMS

All About Me

Hi, my name is Lily and this is a poem about me.
I would describe myself as dark, strange, a bit creepy.
We have multiple skulls. Yes, you heard that right.
We have about three human skulls, one horse, cat, dog, taxidermy things.
Anyway going off that topic now!

My hobby is gymnastics, I do it every day of the week,
Apart from Fridays and Sundays.
I have been doing gym for three years now!
I have done three to four competitions.
One gym-fusion which is gym with dance.
Over the time of Covid,
I have missed five comps and three gym-fusion ones.
I have two comps coming up soon.
I am so excited!

Lily Hubbard (10)
Adcote School For Girls, Little Ness

Decisions

The first decision I had to make,
Was choosing between swimming and cricket.
So I decided to get a cricket and a fish to race.
The cricket won, so I did cricket.
A couple of years later,
I had to choose between ballet and gym.
Luckily the ballet teacher left,
So I continued with gym.
A hard decision that I make every day,
Is what to eat for lunch, breakfast, and dinner.
Life can be hard at some points.
Life is like an old satellite,
Sometimes it works really well,
And sometimes it's not the best.
But the important thing is that,
It's going to be better more than it is worse.

Emma Barlow (10)
Adcote School For Girls, Little Ness

If My Thoughts Were A Person

If my thoughts were a person,
They would read all day.
They would read every book.
While eating lots of food.

If my thoughts were a person,
They would try all the sports.
They would go cycling.
They would play tennis.

If my thoughts were a person,
They would have pasta for lunch,
Chocolate waffles for breakfast,
With ice cream for dessert.

If my thoughts were a person,
They would wander off to daydream,
And then play the guitar,
Cuddling bonobos in the zoo!

Seren Serjeant (10)
Adcote School For Girls, Little Ness

All About Me

T ianna is one of a kind.
I s always including all of her friends.
A nd really loves to ride on her pony.
N ever having enough friends.
N othing will stop her when,
A ny challenge is in front of her, not even her amazing

J ive but a real challenge too.
O nly focus on others and to
N ever just thinks of herself.
E veryone is a friend to her and
S omeday she will chase her dreams of being a photographer.

Tianna Jones (10)
Adcote School For Girls, Little Ness

Unstoppable, Amazing, Wonderful Me!

When you look at me, what do you see?
Kindness, leadership, confidence maybe?
Or maybe you can see a secret talent in me?
Ballet, drama, smiling - definitely!
But maybe you rate me from the outside of me?
My fashion, make-up, hair - really?
No matter how you rate me,
I'm still going to be,
Wonderful, confident, smiley me!
Because no matter how grey my hair is,
Or how arched my back is,
No one can stop unstoppable, amazing,
Wonderful me!

Imogen Buckle (10)
Adcote School For Girls, Little Ness

Jessie Recipe

First, collect 2kg of art and sewing,
Next, add a pinch of marshmallows.
Then add 5kg of unicorns and Disney,
Next, collect 100 grams of butterflies.
Then add some pink and glitter.
Next, stir it all up.
Then add 1kg of reading.
Next, add 1,000,000kg of happiness.
And don't forget the 72g of music.
Lastly, don't forget the pets Daz, Raya,
Sisu, Kitcat, Sapphire and Shadow.
You have found Jessie!

Jessie Senior (10)
Adcote School For Girls, Little Ness

Bea Rose

B eautiful, kind and happy
E ngagement in art and textiles
A chievement in my sport.

R esilience in my maths,
O bservant in my singing,
S ensible in my lessons.
E asy to talk to.

Bea Taylor (10)
Adcote School For Girls, Little Ness

Meet Jasmine

Have you met Jasmine?
Her favourite colour is rose gold.
She loves koalas, pandas and dogs.
She always loves drawing.
Have you met Jasmine?
Her favourite food is pasta.
When she grows up, she'll be a film director!

Jasmine Seago (10)
Adcote School For Girls, Little Ness

Tiger

A haiku

Tiger, hungry eyes
Scanning the wide horizon
Searching for their prey.

Rosanna Jones (10)
Adcote School For Girls, Little Ness

This Is Me

F lexible and funny all day long
R esponsible and cool at singing a song
E xcellent at everything so my teacher says
Y oung at heart nearly most days
A wesome, amazing, this is me

T alented and tidy especially my bedroom
H appy and helpful to my family I am
I nterested in art, books and swimming too
S uper kind and shy but sometimes silent

I nspiring, so my friends tell me
S ometimes sarcastic and silly I love to be

M essy but not often
E xcellent, I try my best

Freya De Stac (8)
Bunscoil Cholmcille, Derry City

This Is Me

T alented at a lot of things.
H opeful and a helpful friend.
I like art.
S uper cheerful and happy.

I make the impossible possible.
S mart, cheerful and happy.

M indful and peaceful.
E ndlessly drawing.

L aughing all the time.
I was born in December.
L ily is my name.
Y lil is my name backwards.

Lily Holland (8)
Bunscoil Cholmcille, Derry City

This Is Me

C onfident.
O utstanding.
B elievable.
H elpful.
L ovely.
A wesome and amazing.
I nspiring.
T alented.
H ard-working.

D rawing and painting.
O ctober is my birthday,
B ooking a party,
B us to get there.
I nspiring again,
N ovember and December.
S anta is coming soon.

Cobhlaith Ní Dhoibn (8)
Bunscoil Cholmcille, Derry City

This Is Me

T he house I live in is over 20 years old
H i, my name is Charlie
I like football, it's the best sport in the world
S even is my favourite number.

I think Manchester United is the best football team
S ome friends are good at football, some aren't.

M y favourite team is Derry City FC
E verybody in my house likes me.

Charlie Mac Cearin Rogan (8)
Bunscoil Cholmcille, Derry City

This Is Me

E mily is my name, sometimes I can be silly.
M y name sounds like it starts with an 'M' but it begins with an 'E'.
I am going to be an artist when I grow up.
L ily is my cousin; we fight a lot but we are still cousins.
Y ou are not the same as me, we are all different.

Emily Niocaill (9)
Bunscoil Cholmcille, Derry City

This Is Me

T alented at horse riding.
H elping my friends.
I nside I like colouring.
S hy and caring.

I nspiring and friendly.
S miling and fun.

M essy and hardworking.
E nd of poem.

Amelia Labhra Tren (8)
Bunscoil Cholmcille, Derry City

This Is Me

I am talented
I like to help people
I am so kind
Sometimes I help my friends

I am a good friend
I am a superhero to my mammy
My mammy is my superhero
Even if I make a robot my mammy said, "That's impressive."
Day and night I play football.

AJ O Chearúil (9)
Bunscoil Cholmcille, Derry City

This Is Me

T alented, this is me,
H appy and hopeful,
I nterested and curious,
S uper kind,

I nspiring to all,
S uper awesome,

M essy but mindful,
E ndless happiness.

Ciarnan O'Duda-O'Baoill (8)
Bunscoil Cholmcille, Derry City

This Is Me

C reative
A wesome
H elpful
I maginative
R adiant at Gaeilge

B rave
O ne of four siblings
Y ou and me get along
L ikeable
E xcellent.

Cahir Ó Baoill (8)
Bunscoil Cholmcille, Derry City

This Is Me

I know loads of facts about animals.

A mazing, friendly and autistic.
M y dog is big.

L ove to make things.
E very day I feed my pets.
O h, I do like video games.

Leo Mac Bhloscaigh (8)
Bunscoil Cholmcille, Derry City

This Is Me

T houghtful.
H appy.
I ndependent sometimes.
S mart too.

I nspired often.
S uper nice.

M e is who I am.
E xcited, sometimes a lot.

Jonah Feeney (8)
Bunscoil Cholmcille, Derry City

This Is Me

M essy and random
A ngry and sad
T ad bit lazy
T ad bit excited
H appy all day
E xploring at the weekend
W hen I eat apples, I go red.

Matthew Hutcheon (8)
Bunscoil Cholmcille, Derry City

This Is Me

R obots are sometimes smart.
O ctopuses have eight tentacles.
N ever tell a lie.
A t the beach, I have lots of fun
N ow it's time to go home.

Rónán Ó Daoighaire (8)
Bunscoil Cholmcille, Derry City

This Is Me

D oing good work.
A ll-day long from nine to three.
R iding my bike with my mammy is fun.
A wesome, friendly, artistic and amazing.

Dara Ó hAilpín (8)
Bunscoil Cholmcille, Derry City

This Is Me

I am happy.
I am fun.
I like the sun.
I like to play with my best friend.
I have lots of friends.

Charlie Harrigan (9)
Bunscoil Cholmcille, Derry City

Feathered Flamingo

I'm a pink feathery flamingo.
Cool.
Amazing.
Long pointy beak.
Cute with long thin legs.
Flat feet, hidden in the water.

Tatiya Nudchanad (8)
Cromer Junior School, Cromer

Poetry Me

Whenever you challenge me,
I will always try to win.
I try my best.
Push myself,
And never give up.
To make my mum proud.

Patryk Imienionek (9)
Cromer Junior School, Cromer

This Is Me!

My name is Subhan.
I have great and loyal friends.
My best friend is called Rayhane.
I enjoy drinking soup and eating chicken.
I appreciate the flavour and taste of rice.
I like to play basketball.
When I go to high school,
I'm willing to join the basketball team,
Along with my best friends.
My friends entertain me a lot.
I appreciate the time they spend with me.
My parents are the best,
They guide me through life.
They make me do stuff that I don't want to do,
But I know they do it for me to understand discipline.
I appreciate everyone,
My friends, my parents.
I am having a great life!
This is me!

Subhan Akram (11)
Cuthbertson Primary School, Glasgow

All About Me

My name is Maryam
And I'm in P7C.
I have the most wonderful teacher
As wonderful as it can be.
I have lots of friends at school with me
That like running and jumping and having fun with me.

I live in Scotland
Where in summer the weather is basically boiling
And in winter the weather is primarily piercing
But both temperatures are unique.

I love baking
It is my favourite thing to do
At least when I'm not reading
Those are the things I do.

People say I inspire an intelligent mind
With knowledge and truth and of course humankind
But nobody is perfect as some try to be
Everyone's unique so just let it be.

My favourite subjects are writing and science
They both are easy but I could use some guidance.
Art isn't really my best strength
'Cause I'm not that straight
But with whatever I do I try my best.

My school's name is Cuthbertson Primary
However, I'm soon going to change it to
Shawlands Academy
'Cause it is my last year until I move to high school.
I'm nervous and excited all at the same time
I just hope it won't turn out as a big whirlpool
I'm sure that won't happen
But I will have a chill through my spine!

Maryam Shaikh (11)
Cuthbertson Primary School, Glasgow

This Is Me!

I've not experienced my full life, there is so much to explore.
I do games, I do sports and I like having fun.
I don't like writing, my strength is maths.
My dream is to become an engineer.
Homework is boring, it's my opinion.
I'm not very creative, my imagination is blank.
I do lots of clubs, I like music.
I play the oboe and enjoy it.
I'm quite nervous going in front of people.
This is me, all you need to know!

Rehan Azher (11)
Cuthbertson Primary School, Glasgow

This Is Me

I am from Scotland in a city named Glasgow.
I like my bed.
I like my books.
I like to sleep.
I like to eat.
And I specifically love cookies,
And tea.
I love to paint
And love to draw.
I like my friends,
Especially my best friends.
I like to have challenges with my friends.
I love my family.
I love to cook my homemade macaroni
With the chicken strips.
This is me.

Raniaa Sheikh (11)
Cuthbertson Primary School, Glasgow

I Am Who I Am

I am who I am.
I want to be what I want to be.
Nobody can stop me.
I won't waste my lifetime.
I want to live my life.
I am a young boy,
Happily enjoying my life.
I am eleven years old and
I don't like the cold.
I've never been exposed,
And I am an honest person.
I am German.
And I want to be a surgeon.
I love the sun,
And my life story has begun...

Yaser Ahmed (11)
Cuthbertson Primary School, Glasgow

Myself

I find being what I want to be,
A coward, an idiot is not in my vocabulary,
Immature, jokester and self-loving, that's me.
Successful in life and be an independent woman,
Don't need to wait on anybody except me.
I am educated and know what I'm doing,
Know where I came from and know what I am doing.
I walk with class, not a frown,
Smart and worthy and I stand my ground.

Amal Abukar (11)
Cuthbertson Primary School, Glasgow

I Am What I Want To Be

I do what I want and I don't let others decide for me.
I am creative and good at what I do.
I am ten years old and I am a boy.
I live in Scotland and I go to school.
I do not give up easily and keep on going.
I am good at drawing and I like to play sports.
I do not care about others telling me what to do.
Overall, I am me and I will always be who I am,
And what I want to be.

Shameer Basra (11)
Cuthbertson Primary School, Glasgow

This Is Me

Rather more to get on about my life.
My hobby is football, I'm as sporty as a sweaty cheetah.
I'm athletic and healthy but my favourite is football.
I'm changing every second.
Making my life an enjoyment.
Let's go football!
I'm on top.
Getting better every minute.
Welcome to my experience,
Of my athletic football hobby.
Bye-bye. This is me!

Sohail Sollehe (11)
Cuthbertson Primary School, Glasgow

Myself

I'm short.
My friends are tall.
My favourite dessert is ice cream.
I'm ten years old.
I wake up late.
I'm a late riser.
I like cats,
But I prefer dogs.
I'm a Sagittarius.
My favourite colour is black.
I don't really like maths.
I'm not the smartest.
Or the fastest but...
I am me.

Denisa Rostas (10)
Cuthbertson Primary School, Glasgow

All About Me

Athletic, however lazy.
Takes losing hard, always comes back.
Enjoys time with friends, sports and more.
When having fun, my happiness soars.
Plays video games quite a lot.
Succeeds in getting bored easily.
Has a delight in new dishes on the plate.
Furthermore hates to skate.
Who is this we speak of?
That would be me.

Rayhane Duarte (11)
Cuthbertson Primary School, Glasgow

This Is Me

I'm furious and ferocious.
I'm full of curiosity and adventures.
Whatever annoys me, I won't keep crying, I'll keep fighting.
I'm full of kindness and shyness.
I really like animals but they have to be mammals.
My favourite sport is basketball.
I'm being me.
This is me.
I'm a superstar striker.

Ali Haider (11)
Cuthbertson Primary School, Glasgow

Honesty Matters To Me

H elpful when someone is sad.
O utgoing to face my fear of heights.
N ice to play games with people.
E asy-going to play nice games.
S porty when I play football or basketball.
T rustworthy when someone tells me something, I don't tell.
Y ou know to count on me.

Zara Munir (11)
Cuthbertson Primary School, Glasgow

This Is Me

I am Hajira Ameer.
I love animals but I'm scared of them too.
I speak and write many languages.
And I've got glasses too.
I have my wonderful teacher and I like her.
I like to play with my friends and with my sisters.
I like to read books.
When I grow up I want to be a doctor.
This is me.

Hajira Ameer (11)
Cuthbertson Primary School, Glasgow

Life

Comes royally at call.
Helps you when you fall.
Fierce like an eagle.
Humble like a beagle.
Lively like a kitten.
Not one that wears mittens.
Forgiven, forgotten.
Rarely frightened.
Loyal and fun.
Royal and done.
Forever loved.
Never stunned.
But this is me.

Hala Alfadel (11)
Cuthbertson Primary School, Glasgow

This Is Me

T actical and fast.
H yper and vast.
I nvincible to any attacks.
S o in love with the colour black.

I magination is my talent.
S uper gallant. Oh, yes I am.

M ilo is my fantastic name.
E nergetic is what I became.

Milo Wisz (11)
Cuthbertson Primary School, Glasgow

This Is Me

This is me.
I love my life.
I love my world
And my whole family.
I love to learn.
I love to read.
I love my home,
Our beautiful planet Earth.
I'm not the fastest
Or the smartest,
But I am myself
And I will always try to be my very best.

Sarah Majid (11)
Cuthbertson Primary School, Glasgow

This Is Me

I like to play games on my PlayStation.
Pizza is my favourite food.
My friend is Adnan (my cousin).
My name is Abdul Rehman, last name Khan.
I'm from a far place called Pakistan but I'm Scottish.
My favourite subject is Art and I dislike Maths.

Abdul Rehman Khan (11)
Cuthbertson Primary School, Glasgow

This Is Me

I love to write.
I love to draw.
I love my family.
I love to learn.
I am a simple girl.
I am brave
And chatty.
Sometimes quite annoying,
But not much.
I get bored when I
Do too much work.
I am friendly as a kitten.

Hania Fatima (11)
Cuthbertson Primary School, Glasgow

This Is Me

My name is Faryal,
My favourite colour is blue,
And maybe pink too.
I am cool just like you.
I am happy for you to be part of the crew.
Yes, me too.
Sometimes I feel blue.
It happens to everyone too.

Faryal Sheikh (11)
Cuthbertson Primary School, Glasgow

This Is Me

My favourite food is noodles and chicken nuggets.
My favoured thing to play is gorilla tag.
My zodiac sign is Cancer.
My favourite thing to watch is anime.
My favourite animals are sloths.
This is me.

Ryan Meggatt (11)
Cuthbertson Primary School, Glasgow

This Is Me

I am sporty.
I'm an artist.
I can cycle and
Recycle.
I like games.
I like a variety of music.
I hate beans.
I love mac and cheese.
I love the outdoors.
This is me.

Awais Hassan (11)
Cuthbertson Primary School, Glasgow

My Favourite Animal

My favourite animal has features:
My favourite animal has big teeth.
My favourite animal has a lot of feathers.
My favourite animal has very sharp nails.
My favourite animal is very strong.

Saad Muhammad Saad (11)
Cuthbertson Primary School, Glasgow

This Is Me

This is me.
My name is Raham.
I love animals.
I love my family.
I am good at drawing animals.
That's my favourite thing to do.
I like mango.
I really like dogs.

Raham Ibrahim (11)
Cuthbertson Primary School, Glasgow

This Is Me

I like to write
I like to bake
I like to draw
I like to paint

I like to read
The books on my shelf
But most of all...
I like to be myself!

Maja Podwika (10)
Cuthbertson Primary School, Glasgow

This Is A Poem About Me

I'm Haider and I'm a boy, young and free,
My name means lion, can't you see?
I grew up as a young cheeky boy,
I loved every single minute - what a joy!
I had a lot of fun under the sun,
Always ended up tired because I can't run!
Hungry now it's time to eat,
Time to wash up and then take a seat,
Pizza is here and it's food time,
Wash it down with a 7UP lemon and lime,
Sit back, relax, play a game of 'Brawl Stars'
My gaming skills are from another planet, maybe
Mars!
What a life,
What a day,
Time now to sit back and lay,
Turn off the lights,
Tomorrow is a new day.

Haider Ali
Dallow Primary School, Luton

My Favourite Thing About Me

My favourite thing about me is,
I am doing my best,
And always taking enough rest!
I want to become a pilot,
So I will work hard - a lot!
When I am sad,
I stay with my mum and dad,
For that, I am very glad.
When I saw Palace Pier at Brighton,
It made me feel very frightened.
I know someone who is very funny,
Because he wants to get lots of money,
But not me, no way.
I just want to become a pilot
So I will work hard - a lot!
And that's my favourite thing about me!

Ismey Shaqur Ayush
Dallow Primary School, Luton

A Poem About Me

I am about as certain as I can be,
That all of us, to some degree,
Have things that even we don't see,
I wonder what I'm yet to learn about me?
I know I'm not the person that I will be tomorrow,
Nor the me from the past,
Shaped by the days that followed,
I'm here in the moment, that's all I can be,
And that's all I can say about me.

Laila Ali Khan (11)
Dallow Primary School, Luton

Split Emotions

As shy as a black butterfly,
Aimlessly drifting through the lanes of a dimmed sky,
Spirit blown away by a gust of negativity,
Like the burned hazel autumnal leaves,
My hands are now worn from all these years,
Now the only thing left in my blank mind is hope,
The only way my mind will cope,
Is to lift my despairing spirit up.

Mysha Ferdous
Dallow Primary School, Luton

What Makes Me

I love to read,
Because it makes my day,
And when I have read,
I see rainbows in my head,
Colours filling the world around me,
When I read,
I feel like I'm on an island,
My book is my friend,
When I read,
The waves of worries,
Are washed away,
I love to read.

Hamidah Odunuga
Dallow Primary School, Luton

Christmas

I love Christmas because it is really fun and you get a lot of presents.
I like dirt bikes, and I wish for one for Christmas.
I like the pigs in blankets and roast beef from Christmas dinner.
I like going outside in the snowy air, like walking in a cold freezer.
I like the early mornings when we wake up at 2am to open our presents.
Me and my mum are up until midnight.

Tommy Chapman (10)
Didcot Primary Academy, Didcot

I May Not Be Perfect, But Really No One Is

I may not be perfect, but really no one is.
I'm unique, I'm diverse, I'm different, I'm a contrast and I'm distinct.
I have both bad and good qualities.
Here are mine: I'm impatient, I worry a lot, I'm not resilient.
I make mistakes, and more.
These don't make me a bad person, but they make me human.
I have many good qualities too.
I'm loyal, beautiful, ambitious, confident and I try to be honest.
I have wonderful friends and a faithful family.
Spectacular animals that care and love me dearly.
I love the eco world, dancing and singing.
I am as brave as a lion.
I am as elegant as a gazelle.
I am as kind as a chimpanzee.
My hair is like a silk sunset,
My eyes like the ocean,

My lips like a rose,
My skin is like porcelain.
This is me!

Bella Vincent-Pink (10)
Didcot Primary Academy, Didcot

This Is Me

Energetic and kind,
And funny, at least within my mind.
Long flowing brown hair,
And loves the fresh air.
Smart as an owl,
I find sprouts foul.
A singer I shall be,
I will relax by the sea,
And my name means jewel.
I am never cruel.
As timid as a mouse,
I like being in my house.
I'll laugh to the end,
But none of this would be true without my best friend.

Amber Hearn (11)
Didcot Primary Academy, Didcot

This Is Me

Short brown curly hair dancing in the wind,
Hazel brown eyes staring at a tree,
Long legs, long arms, sat and folded in the grass.
Round face, red lips, talking to a friend.
Sat down in a place that's comfortable for me.
Picnics are my favourite things.
And that makes me me!

Rotem Wolchinsky
Didcot Primary Academy, Didcot

This Is Me

A guitar lover.
A Magnum muncher.
A Guns 'n' Roses learner.
A pizza gobbler.
A running champion.
A game-changer.
A cat cuddler.
A football god.
A football curver.
A Fortnite pro.
A GTA5 god.
A money earner.
A nine-year-old grower.
A pumpkin carver.

Reuben Urquhart (9)
Edderton Primary School, Tain

This Is Me

A basketball baller.
A chocolate chomper.
A crystal champion.
An eagle explorer.
A family former.
A make-up mother.
A Minecraft miner.
A shell shaker.
A Snapchat snapper.
A Roblox runner.

Evie Bethel (10)
Edderton Primary School, Tain

This Is Me

A TikTok triumph.
An Instagram invader.
A rainbow ruler.
An artistic animal.
A Snapchat snatcher.
A cat catcher.
A Coke cruncher.
A Christmas conqueror.

Tiana Cowie
Edderton Primary School, Tain

This Is Me

A sunshine seer.
A cake creator.
A make-up marvel.
An ice cream eater.
A pizza perfectionist.
A TikTok tester.
A bed bug.
A family favourite.
A fun friend.

Lauren Perks (11)
Edderton Primary School, Tain

This Is Me!

A TV binger.
A football freestyler.
An ice cream enthusiast.
A TikTok trespasser.
A walking worshipper.
A sunset sensation.
A telly terror.

Tyler Parker (11)
Edderton Primary School, Tain

This Is Me

A cat carer.
A tree climber.
A shell seeker.
A dog lover.
An art doer.
A bird watcher.
A movie seer.

William Pearson (11)
Edderton Primary School, Tain

Colours Of Nature

Purple
Butterflies and flowers are
Purple and
Radishes too

Blue
Blue skies and blue seas
And blueberries
Indeed

Green
Grass and leaves
Green
Peacock feathers
Green and nature
Everywhere to see

Yellow
The sun is yellow
And the pollen
From the buttercups
Yellow and a few birdy feathers too

Orange
Orange oranges
On trees
And sunsets in the evening
Beautiful indeed

Red
Red is another blend of the sunset
Beautiful too
Poppy fields remembering the fallen
And including robins' tumtums too

We have finished the
Colours of the rainbow but
What about the other colours...?

Pink
Worms and dragonfruit pink
And pink flamingos
In the tropical seas

White
Snow and clouds is a
Nice plain colour

And add a bit of the darkness you have...

Grey
Grey stones
Grey mountains
And grey pigeons
And the moon

Black
The night sky is black
And the little beetles
Crawling in the bushes in the black

Peach
Salmon and a parrot
And peach
And the sand

Nature is beautiful, it is life
Nature is us
Nature is crumbling apart
There is no Earth 2
But we can change

Help the Earth!

Emily Waller (10)
Evendons Primary School, Wokingham

Best Friends

'One hand in mine, my hand in thine,
We walk through life's stark shadow,
Two as one and one combine,
To fight the night's battle.'

Together we shall be, never apart, never alone,
Within our heart, we have our zone,
We fall alone but rise together,
A never-ending friendship is in our wake,
We reign this city, it's ours to be free.

Together forever in harmony,
Free and wild.
Long grass tickles our legs as we run,
We giggle alone in the shade of a tree,
Climbing high and low hand in hand,
This is our land, we run free

So far away from the sea but who cares,
We climb the world's hard stairs,
United and together forever,
Back to the forest we go.

Rosie Smallhorne (10)
Evendons Primary School, Wokingham

This Is Me, Thomas

I am Thomas,
I'm sometimes called Tommo or Tommy,
But my favourite is when I'm called Uncle Tom.

Now on to me,
I am 145cm tall,
With eyes a deep brown - as dark as the soil on the ground.

My hair is dark blonde,
With curls that come through,
When I let it grow long, which I don't often do!

You can always identify me,
By the mole on my face,
You can't help but see.

Food for me is pretty plain,
But give me a roast dinner with plenty of Yorkshires,
And filled to the brim with awesome gravy.

I love my Nerf guns,
They are powerful, dynamic and shoot way too far,

So end up spending hours retrieving the bullets from my backyard.

Pokémon cards are the best,
My favourite is Rainbow Rare Glaceon,
I occasionally look at it and when I do, it glistens, glows and shines in the sun.

I love sports.
Football - I just love kicking the ball super far,
I love being on the pitch but will never say no to helping the team save a goal.

I love fast cars,
And if I had to choose one to represent me,
It would be a Lamborghini - fast, sleek and just a stunning machine.

Finally - I'm funny and kind.
Sometimes a pain.

But that's what makes me *me*!

Thomas Caster (10)
Evendons Primary School, Wokingham

I Live In Aggieland

I live in Aggieland.
Aggieland is purple and filled with snow
It's the very best place to be.
It's free from parents
And no siblings.
It's got its own language - Maniwaching.
That means, hey, no one can come here,
It's just me and my dog and my world around here.
The books are huge to really step in,
Dog kennels are the size of mountains,
There are about ten trillion chocolate fountains,
And pizza slices have legs that are running.
There's no one to catch me raiding the biscuit tin!

If you want to live in Aggieland, you can't just pack and go,
It's much harder than that, I think that you should know,
You'll have to draw a sausage roll terrorising you,
In a book about a Flareon that turned into Mew.
You'll have to find a Curly-Wurly that will also come to life

And be as merry as a cherry.
Only then will you know that you'll be in Aggieland.
And then after that, you'll be as small as a mouse
And ice skate all the way to my house...

"Agnes? Agnes?!"
"Huh?"
"What's 4767 minus 2459?"
"Ummmm..."
"You really need to stop being in Aggieland."

Agnes Clayton (11)
Evendons Primary School, Wokingham

This Is Me!

Terrifically awesome, I cannot be stopped,
My craziness explodes like I have just been popped,
My guinea pig is called Rose,
She and I like to strike a pose.
Hannah is my name,
Drama is my game,
I'm a drama queen,
And I love to be seen.
I live with my mum, my brother, my piggies and my dad,
Spending time with them usually makes me glad,
I have a nine-year-old brother called Scott,
Video games he plays a lot.
Super smart,
I've got a big heart,
I'm caring and kind,
I've got a good mind.
I like to bake,
Cookies, crumbles, bread and cake,
I don't eat meat,
And I like a good sweet.

So I like food, animals, sweets, but what more?
Reading, writing, over books I pore,
I like Guides and martial arts and in drama class,
I get the best parts.
Magnificent and cool,
I am quite tall,
Brown hair and eyes,
It's no surprise.
Evendons is my school,
I think some of the lessons are cool,
I'm the oldest child there,
For the little ones I really care.

Hannah Nascimento (11)
Evendons Primary School, Wokingham

My Life And Me

This is me,
My eyes are as blue as the sky,
I really wish I could fly,
In my dreams,
I wish I had ice cream,
I love sour sweets,
And sweet treats,
I love food and fashion,
I like playing with Lego,
I wish I had a pet panda called Hugo,
I love playing video games,
I really wish I was on the wall of fame,
My hair is as dark as night,
My face is as bright as the light,
I like different holidays like Christmas, Halloween, Valentine's Day, Easter, Pancake Day and my birthday,
I am funny, kind, smart, my friends say I am brave,
My fave colour is purple and that is the colour of our school,
My hobby is reading,

My fave animal is a panda,
I love BTS, they're the best band ever!
My zodiac sign is Virgo,
My fave subject is English,
I am sort of fast at typing,
But I am good at touch typing,
This is me.

Evelyn Chandler (9)
Evendons Primary School, Wokingham

This Is Who I Am

Jofra Archer and James Vince are my idols,
Yet lies and cheats are my rivals,
I like cricket, tennis and ACDC,
This is me.

I have hopes and dreams beyond imagination,
They're full of light, colour and creation,
I wish to be a writer,
And make my future even brighter.

Nibbles and Florence are my pets,
And maybe someday I could become a vet,
Robins, blue tits and birds of all sorts,
They give me support.

Autumn is my favourite season,
I do have a reason,
The colours of the leaves, amber and fire,
As happiness flies higher and higher.

Christmas is all so near,
It makes me want to cheer,

The feeling of it makes me excited,
While some people are kind of delighted.

To end this poem about me,
I just want to say,
This is who I want to be,
And this is how I want to stay.

Lucy Didcock (10)
Evendons Primary School, Wokingham

This Is Me!

I need to write a poem that is all about me, so I look in the mirror and what can I see?
I see hair thick and curly, coloured light brown and a face that looks happy when I try not to frown.
I see eyes that shine brightly and a mouth that smiles nicely.
I see a girl that is kind and thinks straight from her mind.
I see a girl with one hamster and two fluffy cats, a girl who will try to do well in her SATs.
I see a girl who loves horses and she's learning to ride, when she does well she has a glow full of pride.
When I look in the mirror I see that I'm tall, to measure my height I stand by my wall.
I see a girl who has to try not to fidget, even though her age is double-digits.
So really I think I like what I see and this is the end of the poem about me.

Viola Williams (10)
Evendons Primary School, Wokingham

My Lovely Life!

I am a lightning bolt in typing.
I have eyes dark as midnight.
I am a panda lover,
I love Christmas and Halloween, Easter,
Valentine's, Pancake Day and my birthday.
My favourite thing to do is gaming and playing with my friends.
My hair is as dark as the night.
When I am older I want to be a vet,
And help the animals in need.
I am a chatterbox about pandas.
I wish I had a pet panda called Mico.
My favourite animal is a panda.
My favourite food is... pizza!
My favourite subject is maths.
I am kind, funny and sometimes weird,
My friends say I am really fast at typing.
My favourite singer is Ariana Grande.
My favourite colours are purple and blue.
This is me!

Sienna Gill (8)
Evendons Primary School, Wokingham

This Is Me

I'm definitely not normal,
Not similar nor different.
I am curious, fun and friendly,
Artistic and a bit stubborn too!
I am polite (sort of!).
Hi! How are you?

I am definitely not normal,
Not similar nor different.
I can be messy,
Fearless and adventurous,
Trying new things all the time!

I am definitely not normal,
Not similar nor different.
I have my bad qualities too!
I can get angry,
Sad or lonely!
Don't worry (that's my job),
I get over them quickly!

My hair can be a mess,
My eyes are a sea of green.
My lips a shade of pink,
My uniform is the same.
And that, my reader, that is me!

Jennifer Sharpe (10)
Evendons Primary School, Wokingham

This Is Me

My name is Max, this poem's about me,
I am 10 and I go to Evendons Primary.
I live on the 'Finch', close to school,
I walk by myself which I think is cool.
I love to eat pizza, Hawaiian's my fave,
Pineapple on pizza? Try it, be brave.
I like to play games and watch films on TV,
"Turn it down," shout my parents, "it's far too noisy."
My sister's called Elin, her work is quite far,
But she doesn't mind, she has a new car.
My mum is a nurse, she looks after the sick,
My dad's an engineer and knows how things tick.
They both love their jobs, each other and me.
My name is Max and I'm very happy.

Max Williams (10)
Evendons Primary School, Wokingham

Animals Around Me

Wherever I go an animal will always follow,
Whether it's a cat, a rat or even a flamingo,
I do not ask these dogs to follow me wherever I go,
But of course, they will follow me home (oh no).
Inside my house there are mice but at least there aren't lions or hawks,
Oh wait, I spoke too soon and they popped all my balloons,
I guess I'll have to get more at the grocery store,
As soon as I can get this boar to just stop following me,
And now this meerkat is drinking all my amazing tea,
I just want peace and quietness from all these animals,
Oh wait, I have an idea, all I need to do is feed these animals food
And they will leave me alone finally.

Evelyn Shanahan (10)
Evendons Primary School, Wokingham

The Flying Dog Turtle

F lying through the sky,
L ighting his path,
Y earning for someone to see him,
I n the dark sky,
N ever had he been seen before,
G etting closer to the ground.

D aylight rose,
O ver the hills,
G reat mysteries surrounded,

T he Flying Dog Turtle and his mysterious wings.
U ntil one special day,
R ight before a little boy's eyes,
T he magical wings opened up and were as colourful as a rainbow,
L anding on the fresh, lush grass,
E nding the mystery surrounding the Flying Dog Turtle.

Joseph Sanchez (10)
Evendons Primary School, Wokingham

I Am Me

I like animals such as dogs, cats and horses.
I love eating sausage rolls, strawberries and fudge.
I am a funny, fabulous friend.
I am also as fast as a cheetah.
Sometimes I feel like being all perfect, you know.
Sometimes I just feel too lazy, you know.
One of my dreams is to fly in the sky very high.
The other one is to live in a world full of sweets.
I like calming myself by going outside or relaxing on the beach and going in the sea.
My favourite thing about me is that I am different from everyone.
Everybody is special whether they are a friend or not.
But my favourite thing of all is I am me!

Emma Steiner (8)
Evendons Primary School, Wokingham

This Is Me - Oscar Thackrah

Oscar's my name,
And soon I shall have fame.
I can be obedient, but stubborn to some,
You'll see me in a McLaren, hear it hum.
Small but mighty, size doesn't matter,
When I see my friend, all I do is chatter.
I can be chaotic, but my heart is in the right place,
You'll know it for real when you see me face to face.
Always moving and having fun,
Got to keep healthy so I light up like the sun.
Running around, playing sports that's what I'm for,
Never knew I was good at it until I asked for more.
But for now, I'm just a kid.
This is me,
Oscar.

Oscar Thackrah (10)
Evendons Primary School, Wokingham

About Me

There's always a battle going on in my brain,
Of likes and dislikes again and again,
Sometimes I like things,
And sometimes I don't,
Like homework and maths,
But sometimes I won't,
Like bananas, beans and potato that's mashed,
And people who litter with rubbish and trash.

I like doing art, I find it relaxing,
Movies and gaming whilst I'm chillaxing,
I love playing sport and like to play magic,
With playing cards, coins and bits of elastic,
My most favourite things are my pets when I'm
home,
They make me feel happy and never
Alone.

William Sharpe (10)
Evendons Primary School, Wokingham

This Is Me

This is me.
At first, there isn't much to see -
Someone dull and sincere,
But I am more wild than I appear!
I score masses of points in basketball,
Which makes me shout and cheer.
I open heaps of Pokémon packs,
So I end up having stacks and stacks and stacks.
I play video games like no other,
Especially with my little brother.
You may also even find,
That I am particularly kind.
My amazing friends always stick up for me,
No matter what the situation may be.
I am a bit more extraordinary than I may seem.
This is me.

Finley Pears (10)
Evendons Primary School, Wokingham

I Am Nature

I am a cheetah, as fast as lightning,
I am a bird, singing when my doors shut,
I am a wave, crashing into my friends,
I am the sun, warm and kind,
I am a lion, brave and strong,
I am a horse, always hungry,
I am a volcano, erupting when my brother wins against me,
I am a mountain, nothing gets past me,
I am a sloth, always tired,
I am a dog, always playing with a ball,
I am a goat, always trying to get to the highest point,
I am a bat because I love the dark,
I am a deer, normally calm,
I am a giraffe, very tall.
I am Nature.

George Dempsey (9)
Evendons Primary School, Wokingham

If I Could Fly!

If I could fly ever so high up above the trees,
I'd twirl and play and laugh all day and feel the gentle breeze.
I'd spot blue tits, finches and robins galore,
Which would make me feel in total awe.
If I could fly ever so high, I would feel so pure.
If I could fly ever so far, I'd conquer the seven seas,
I'd dive and splash and in a flash, I'd swim with pleasurable ease.
I'd kill serpents, sharks and pirates with glee,
Which would make the mermaids grateful for me.
If I could fly ever so far, I would feel so free.

George Battisson (10)
Evendons Primary School, Wokingham

Magic

Magic is cool, magic is rare, magic can be found anywhere.
It turns and twists into corners and cracks,
Even if you're sad it won't let you slack.
Magic can be cosy, it can feel great,
As long as you keep it warm and keep it safe from other things that are ready to bite.
Keep it safe with all your might.
Could you?
Would you?
Share a little magic in someone's life?
Try to smile at a friend as you go past.
Hold a door open.
You will find that magic spreads fast.
Everybody needs to make that little effort.

Zofia Britton (11)
Evendons Primary School, Wokingham

Shopping All Alone

As I sit and ponder late at night,
I hear the owls twoot in the distance.
I know I should be in bed asleep,
But I just can't wait.

"It's the big day," my mum says,
I could shop with my friends,
No adult in sight.
Just me and my friends all alone
We can shop, eat and have fun.

It's a mixture of emotions, happy,
Excited and scared.
I have not done this before,
What if I get lost?
Or something goes wrong?
What will happen?
Who will help?

Katie Lovell (10)
Evendons Primary School, Wokingham

This Is Me!

T easing is my passion,
H appy is my feeling,
I ndependent is what I am,
S illy is how I act.

I maginative is what my friends call me,
S arcastic is what my sister says I am.

M essy is what I am, but not what I mean to do,
E ila is my name and I am glad about that.

Eila is my name,
I am glad about that and
Don't try to change me,
Glad is my feeling,

Silly is how I act and
I know that for sure.

Eila Foote-Stubban (10)
Evendons Primary School, Wokingham

This Is Me Poem!

I am funny, curious, and kind,
I like puzzles that test my mind,
I enjoy knitting in my room,
And roller skating at noon.

I am passionate about my friends,
I do taekwondo to defend,
Being an author is my dream,
And my writing always gleams.

I dislike pizza, mud, and rain,
It does nothing for my brain,
And homework in my mind,
Is an awful waste of time.

I'm proud and strong,
With awesome songs,
I'm brave and smart,
With awesome art.

Megan Vale (10)
Evendons Primary School, Wokingham

This Is Me

Musical notes brought me up,
They made me dance and fly,
Polish mother and half English father if you ever wondered why,
Mochi is my favourite food, do you have one too?
Games let me play,
I'll fight until the light of day,
My corgi Penny and I,
Love watching anime in the night,
My favourite drink is J2O,
I'm not sure Penny likes it though,
And if I had a job, actress, voice actor, artist and author too,
I don't suppose I could choose,
I wonder, how could you?

Izabela Lanigan (10)
Evendons Primary School, Wokingham

This Is Me

My dream in the future is to be a singer, actor or a pet groomer.
I love delicious dark chocolate.
I love pets like dogs, cats, rabbits, hamsters and guinea pigs.
I eat loads of crisps, especially hot and spicy crisps.
I love the protein pancakes that my mum makes.
I also have a Lego station.
I am a brilliant goalie, I have goalie gloves too.
I am as fast as a ball flying in the air.
I am pearls of wisdom!
My eyes are as blue as the sky, they are as round as a marble.
This is me!

Harriet Cumberland (9)
Evendons Primary School, Wokingham

This Is Me!

I am like a pomeranian,
I am as cute as a pomeranian,
As intelligent as a pomeranian,
As friendly as a pomeranian,
As yappy as a pomeranian,
As social as a pomeranian,
As small as a pomeranian,
As playful as a pomeranian,
As adventurous as a pomeranian,
As... wait,
I am so like a pomeranian, that maybe I am a pomeranian!

I am cute, intelligent, friendly, yappy, social, playful, adventurous, and small, and I think those traits make me the greatest of them all!

Brianna Vale (10)
Evendons Primary School, Wokingham

Football

Running in the wind, passing the ball,
It comes to me again, I won't fall.
As I shoot,
I lose my boot!
The crowd give a big whoop!

Now it's the second half,
I have a chance again,
Running down the wing,
Making the crowd sing.

As I hit the net
My goal is set,
I make the opposition fear
As my family cheer.

The game finishes shortly after,
We all laugh about my disaster,
Next time I will do my laces faster!

James Fish (10)
Evendons Primary School, Wokingham

I Like My Life

I like my life.
I love playing football with my friends at school.
I have got good games at home.
My brother is a kind brother,
He makes fun things for me and lets me have things for free.
My mum is the best mum,
She brings me to funfairs,
She lets me have her tea and makes drinks for me,
She cooks good dinners and gets me to sleep.
My dad is the best dad,
He takes me to town,
He buys me magazines and he takes me down to school.
I like my life.

Leighton Kerr (8)
Evendons Primary School, Wokingham

Who Am I?

I am a helper of who believe in me,
I am a guidance for mankind,
I am a treasure of a righteous person,
I am a ripe fruit for a grateful mortal,
I am a jewel of a man's intellect,
I am comfort for a burdened human,
I am an advocate of who remembers me,
I am vindication on behalf of guilt,
I am a fragrance and aroma of perfume,
I am a revival for the heart,
Some consider my worth like gold,
Who am I then?
Well, it's for you to decide.

Rabia Rizwan (11)
Evendons Primary School, Wokingham

This Is Me

Football is the game for me,
I am the fastest on the team,
I play for Reeves and at school,
The game is so cool!

My other favourite thing to do,
Is play with my cockapoo,
He's only small but very fast,
He loves to run through the grass.

Finally, you'll find me on my PS5,
Exploring stuff and shooting bad guys,
I'm the best in the household,
My parents are rubbish and my dad is bald!

Ethan Olney (10)
Evendons Primary School, Wokingham

I Am Who I Am

I am big.
I am strong.
I am caring, kind and helpful.
I love football and I am a baller in the boots.
I am cheerful and understand when other people are in need.
I love gaming.
I am gentle.
I am rapid like a lightning cheetah.
I am a super striker, scoring most of the goals on the pitch.
I am warming like the sun.
I am funny like a fox, cheering my friends up.
I am who I am and no one can stop me!

Mali Buchanan (8)
Evendons Primary School, Wokingham

This Is Me

My favourite holiday is Christmas.
I like animals, my favourites are cats and bunnies.
My favourite thing to do is laser tag, it's where I let my worries out.
I have five friends, they are called Evelyn, Harriet, Shivi, Emma and finally Jasmine.
When I am sad I like rapping.
My dream is to be a rapper.
When I look at the sunset, it's like a shining crystal on an open river.
My favourite music is BTS.

Millie Ellis (9)
Evendons Primary School, Wokingham

I Am Me

I am the best me.
I am a number crusher.
Candyfloss is my dream.
Guinea pigs are my best friends.
...They squeak at me.
I love lying in bed, especially the wrong way round.
My favourite colour is bluish-purple, it looks quite nice.
My favourite number is 82, it just sounds cool.
I am very sporty, dodgeball rules.
Soft things are my favourite, I love hugging them.

I am me.

Scott Nascimento (9)
Evendons Primary School, Wokingham

All About Me

I like to kick a ball.
But Pokémon I adore all.
I like dogs
And not frogs.
I love to run
But still get my homework done.
I always love to make a pancake cook.
So I also like to pick up and read some books.
I enjoy scoring goals.
I also like animals like foals.
In Minecraft,
I find mine shafts.
I watch YouTube
Whilst eating a Frube.
This is me.

Alex Turner (10)
Evendons Primary School, Wokingham

This Is Me

I love to play with my friends, and what we play depends,
I wish I had a pet, but I haven't got one yet,
I am a brilliant swimmer, and I like to be a winner,
I am one-quarter of my family, but I wish my name was Amalie,
I am a big sister and when she goes away I miss her,
I am mostly very happy, and if I get a dog I don't want it to be yappy,
When I am angry, I can be very cranky.

Annabella Lovell (11)
Evendons Primary School, Wokingham

Football Mad

I love to play football in a team,
Playing for Man United last night was my dream,
I stood out on the field with my heart beating fast,
No one could catch me, I was a blast,
I was suddenly praised,
My coach was amazed,
With my bright blue boot,
I ran up to shoot,
"Goal!" I screamed, it flew in with a thump,
No one could save it,
They were all in a grump.

Oscar Bradbury (10)
Evendons Primary School, Wokingham

The Things That Make Me Tick

The things that make me tick are things like a school trip.
I love to ride my bike, I've even been known to go on a hike.
I play football for a team and after that my shirt needs a clean.
I've always been happy since the days I've been in a nappy.
I have a younger brother who looks like my mother.
I wish I could be a jockey but it looks like I'm stuck with hockey.

Joshua Beighton (10)
Evendons Primary School, Wokingham

The Nature Trail

I am as fast as a cheetah.
My eyes are green like cats.
I look around and see a bat.
My arms spread out like wings.
My brain is as smart as an owl's.
I am an animal lover and family lover and think about my friends.
I love gymnastics, it's my favourite sport.
I teach my friends it at school.
I love my school and all my friends.
This is me and my life.

Daisy Richards (9)
Evendons Primary School, Wokingham

All About Nature

The stream flowed and the wind blew,
The leaves rustled and
The birds cheeped,
The summer was changing,
The sun shone above the clouds,
There was a rainbow and a pot of gold,
And cheetahs ran as fast as lightning,
And the animals were quiet.
It was like a pond and a frog,
It was like a raindrop from the sky,
It was a dark sky,
And it was me.

Ethan Belas (8)
Evendons Primary School, Wokingham

Fantasy Dream

I'm from an alternate universe,
Where dragons and unicorns stay,
I can make anything you want,
Like curses, if you say.

I'm a way to escape (from real life),
Although you can't catch me on tape,

All you have to do is close your eyes,
Think hard and realise,
A dream is a dream in wonderland,
That is all you have to understand.

Natasha Hunter (10)
Evendons Primary School, Wokingham

All About Me!

I'm a girl called Daisy who's ten years old,
I love blue and purple and love to cook,
And I like to sing too.

I play games with my friend and eat pasta too!
I'm chatty and kind with an artistic side,
I like many sports like netball.

I love to sing, dance and play,
But spending time with my family is the best
Time of the day.

Daisy Crowley (10)
Evendons Primary School, Wokingham

This Is Lola

This is me, yo I am Lola
I like to be me
Just perfectly me
I love to play football with my team
My friends and family are loyal to me
Climbing trees is my speciality
My cat Chesnut is not very cuddly
My favourite drink is Fanta
It fizzes and pops in my mouth
I like to act and sing
While swinging in a tree
This is me.

Lola Tate (10)
Evendons Primary School, Wokingham

My Perfect Day

The time has come
"Wake up! Wake up!" says Mum,
Playing in the rain,
Running again and again,
Climbing the hugest tree,
Feeling ever so free.

Ting! 9 o'clock has come,
"Time to go to bed," says my mum,
"I have got a very cosy bed," I said,
So I am happy I am going to bed.

Lily Shambrook (10)
Evendons Primary School, Wokingham

I Am (A) Jem

Curly hair and an infectious giggle,
Never sits still, always needs to wriggle.
Freckled of face,
Can run at a pace.
Loveable underdog, loyal friend,
Smart and kind to the end.
Book worm and dog lover,
Reading history books cover to cover.
Striving to be a scouting adventurer,
Jem by name and a gem by nature.

Jem Jordaan (10)
Evendons Primary School, Wokingham

Gaming

As soon as I turn on my Xbox, I teleport,
Flying and shooting, building and making friends,
I can't get enough of it,
Sometimes I don't know what to play but I will always find one to play,
Sometimes I get a game that I don't really like,
But then I find a new game and I teleport to a whole new world.

Jenson Joyce (10)
Evendons Primary School, Wokingham

Me

I am sporty, an agile midfielder like a serval.
A strong defender, like a tiger.
I am friendly like my tabby cats but sometimes, I get into scraps.
I'm adventurous, I like the woods, climbing trees like a leopard.
I chill like a lion under a tree, lying on the sofa watching TV.
This is my poem all about me!

Isaac Moore (10)
Evendons Primary School, Wokingham

This Is Me

T his is who I am.
H ave many friends also,
I 'm kind, smart and funny,
S imilar to some, animal lover I am.

I 'm a great artist, mentally and physically,
S ometimes sad, sometimes mad,

M e is who I am.
E xcellent at maths.

Nicole Zarwanska (10)
Evendons Primary School, Wokingham

What Skill Am I?

I feel brave, for the moment at least,
I'll turn over every rock,
I'll do what I want,
There's nothing that can stop me,
I'll aim for the top because that's who I am,
I want to reach the top,
I need to reach the top,
I will reach the top,
What skill am I?

Matilda Foote-Stubban (10)
Evendons Primary School, Wokingham

This Is Me

T hankful and grateful,
H yper and energetic,
I nterruptive but great listener,
S ometimes over-reactive.

I ntelligent and smart,
S ometimes too excited.

M aths for me is easy.
E nglish isn't so easy.

Oliver Bratchyk (10)
Evendons Primary School, Wokingham

I Am Who I Am

I look in the mirror,
And what do I see?
I see me,
No one else can be.

My size, my shape,
The colour of my hair.
All make up me,
And I am aware.

I like who I am,
I want to stay.
Don't try to change me,
Or I'll run away.

Evie Granovsky (10)
Evendons Primary School, Wokingham

This Is My Life

I like technology
It's not like biology
My coding is bold
I'm eight years old
I have Lego bricks
They don't come from Wickes
I am a big brother
And I discover
My inventions explode
Making the computer corrode

This is my life!

Isaac Burgess (8)
Evendons Primary School, Wokingham

Amazing Animals

I love animals because they're cute and fluffy.
I like ice cream because it's good for an ice-cold day.
Easter is my favourite time of year because it's exciting.
I like baking brownies every Sunday.
I want to be a vet when I'm older so I can help animals.

Jasmine Turner (8)
Evendons Primary School, Wokingham

Diplodocus

As I stomped through rainforests,
No fear inside at all,
I met kind diplodocus,
One about to fall.
I helped her up,
Getting kind of bored,
So I went to another,
We looked at each other.
All I wanted was to play,
But he turned and ran away.

Adam Stone (10)
Evendons Primary School, Wokingham

What Sport Is It?

The ball goes as fast as lightning,
Some are rough runners, some are not,
But some goals are as high as a skyscraper,
And same are small as a box,
The grass is jumpy or Astro can be as smooth as a tile,
What sport is it?

Answer: Football.

Ariyan Yash Nagar (11)
Evendons Primary School, Wokingham

The Dark Woods

I am as sneaky as a snake.
My eyes are brown marbles.
I have brown silky smooth hair.
I love animals.
I have a cute hamster.
I love my school.
I have eight fish.
I have a sister, she is so cute.

Poppy Knight (8)
Evendons Primary School, Wokingham

This Is Me

T houghtful.
H umble.
I love my cat.
S mart.

I mpossible to convince.
S ometimes funny.

M y friends are fun.
E xcited.

Kornelia Przymecka (10)
Evendons Primary School, Wokingham

Hobbies

I am Floyd,
The one and only,
I am many things but not lonely.
I have family, mates, none of them are fake.
I like coding, hacking, spending time online,
Homework however I always decline!

Floyd Currie (10)
Evendons Primary School, Wokingham

Who Am I?

I am a math lover.
A story reader.
A non-fiction lover.
A card and paper manipulator.
A STEM user.
A GB supporter.
A mountain goat when on a bike.

Who am I?

James Scott (10)
Evendons Primary School, Wokingham

About Me

I like the Lego Movie 2.
I will devour pizza.
I like bright colours.
I like chocolate and ice cream
I watch YouTube and I like it.
My favourite YouTuber is Slogoman.

Daniel Turner (8)
Evendons Primary School, Wokingham

This Is Me, Jackson

J umping jacks.
A xolotl lover.
C aring for cats.
K indness matters.
S impsons lover.
O utstanding.
N ature-loving.

Jackson Williams (10)
Evendons Primary School, Wokingham

Dexter And His Pets

My pets are cute.
They are very fluffy.
They want strokes all the time.
One of my pets hunts and
One of my pets is really friendly.
What are they?

Dexter Gilham-King (10)
Evendons Primary School, Wokingham

This Is Me

I am Toby.
I like playful puppies, delightful desserts and calming cooking shows.
I feel good when I see bright colours.
I have lake green eyes.

Toby Jordaan (8)
Evendons Primary School, Wokingham

YoungWriters Est. 1991

YOUNG WRITERS INFORMATION

We hope you have enjoyed reading this book – and that you will continue to in the coming years.

If you're the parent or family member of an enthusiastic poet or story writer, do visit our website **www.youngwriters.co.uk/subscribe** and sign up to receive news, competitions, writing challenges and tips, activities and much, much more! There's lots to keep budding writers motivated!

If you would like to order further copies of this book, or any of our other titles, then please give us a call or order via your online account.

Young Writers
Remus House
Coltsfoot Drive
Peterborough
PE2 9BF
(01733) 890066
info@youngwriters.co.uk

Join in the conversation!
Tips, news, giveaways and much more!

YoungWritersUK **YoungWritersCW** **youngwriterscw**